By The Grace and Mercy of God
I Made It

By The Grace and Mercy of God
I Made It

by Juanita Crawford, *Ed.D, MSN, RN*

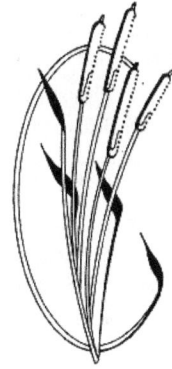

Senior Publisher
Steven Hill

ASA Publishing Corporation

ASA Publishing Corporation
An Accredited Publishing House with the BBB

105 E. Front St., Suite 101
Monroe, Michigan 48161
www.asapublishingcorporation.com

All Rights Reserved. No part of this publication may be reproduced, stored in a retrieval system or transmitted in any form or by any means electronic, mechanical, photocopying, recording or otherwise, without the prior written permission of the publisher. Author/writer rights to "Freedom of Speech" protected by and with the "1st Amendment" of the Constitution of the United States of America. This is a work of Christian beliefs. Any resemblance to actual events, locales, person living or deceased is entirely coincidental. Other names, places, and characters are within the work of biblical knowledge and its entirety is from the ministerial aspects of its author.

Any and all vending sales and distribution not permitted without full book cover and this title page.

Copyrights©2015 Juanita Crawford, All Rights Reserved
Book: By The Grace and Mercy of God I Made It
Date Published: 04.29.14/Edition 1 *Trade Paperback*
Book ASAPCID: 2380672
ISBN: 978-1-886528-95-6
Library of Congress Cataloging-in-Publication Data

This book was published in the United States of America.
State of Michigan

A Publisher Trademark Copy page

TABLE OF CONTENTS

By The Grace and Mercy of God I Made It! ....
    FORWARD i
    DEDICATION iii
    ACKNOWLEDGEMENTS v

CHAPTER 1: INTRODUCTION 1
    Background 2
    Statement of the Uncertainty 5

CHAPTER 2: RAMIFICATIONS OF DISOBEDIENCE 7
    The Miracle 9
    Jesus Still Knocking 11
    A Guided Blessing 24

CHAPTER 3: IMPLICATIONS OF BEING OBEDIENT 27
    Fully Committed 28
    Desires of my Heart 29

CHAPTER 4: HAVOC TIMES 41
    Prospective Change of Heart 42
    Keeping the Faith 45

CHAPTER 5: HOLDING ON 47
    Ignoring Naysayers 47
    God Sometimes Challenge Us 49

CHAPTER 6: EXPECT THE UNEXPECTED 53
    Moving Forward 55
    Experiencing the Grace and Mercy of God 62

CHAPTER 7: RENDERING SERVICES 69
    The Appeal 71
    Conclusions 73

References 79

About The Author 81

FORWARD

FACING TRIALS AND TRIBULATIONS THE DAUGHTER OF THE LATE REV. AND MRS. THOMAS FORD STRIVES TO EXCEL IN RELIGIOUS AS WELL AS SECULAR EDUCATION. ALTHOUGH MANY VOICED SHE WOULD NOT SURPASS THROUGH THIS TEDIOUS JOURNEY, SHE ATTESTS WHILE HOLDING ON WITH MUSTARD SEED FAITH AND ANCHORAGE IN JESUS CHRIST, TRIUMPH WAS THE OUTCOME. "THOU THEREFORE ENDURE HARDNESS, AS A GOOD SOLDIER OF JESUS CHRIST. NO MAN THAT WARRETH ENTANGLETH HIMSELF WITH THE AFFAIRS OF THIS LIFE; THAT HE MAY PLEASE HIM WHO HATH CHOSEN HIM TO BE A SOLDIER. AND IF A MAN ALSO STRIVE FOR MASTERIES, YET IS HE NOT CROWNED, EXCEPT HE STRIVE LAWFULLY" (2ND TIMOTHY 2:3-5).

DEDICATION

This book is dedicated to my parents the late Rev. and Mrs. Thomas Ford who instilled in me the importance of charity, faith, righteousness and education. This book is dedicated to my husband: Rev. Emmett Crawford Jr., my three loving daughters and son-in-laws: Kimberly Rebecca Campbell (Kris), Franita Kenyatta Gathings (Isaiah), Ronda Latricia Suthers (Marcus), my grandchildren , great grandchildren, and my god daughter Desiree Anita Ivory. This book is especially dedicated to my godmother: the late Mrs. Louise Young (my second mother) who has been an inspiration in my life for many years. I dedicate this book to all my siblings, sisters: Ann (deceased), Gwendolyn, Rebecca, Evangelist Theresa Skinner, and Wanda. Brothers: Willie Thomas (deceased), Deacon Cornelius Ford, Rev. David Ford, Mark, Rev. Demetrius Ford, J.D., Ph.D., Psy.D., and Jonathan. I dedicate this book to all my nieces and nephews.

Author's Parents on their Wedding Day
-The Late Rev. & Mrs. Thomas Ford-

ACKNOWLEDGEMENTS

I give reverence to my Lord and Savior Jesus Christ, who guided, encouraged, comforted, and empowered me throughout this tedious journey and for permitting me to write this book. *Heavenly Father, I solely acknowledge that only by Your Grace and Mercy could these tasks have been completed. Thank you Father, for being my refuge and strength, in the present time of difficulty (Psalm 46:1)*

All Scriptures quoted and paraphrased are taken from the Holy Bible (KJV), unless otherwise denoted

By The Grace and Mercy of God
I Made It

by Juanita Crawford, *Ed.D, MSN, RN*

CHAPTER 1
INTRODUCTION

The struggles of life can be challenging for non-Christians as well as Christians. Often one tends to posit that Christians lives are unchallenged; this statement is a fallacy, remember Job, his friends, and their accusations (Job 29-31). While not comparing oneself to Job, my claim is being a born again Christian striving to meet my Savior Jesus Christ while daily facing havoc times (as well as pleasant times) on earth. My stance is that Jesus Christ is the Son of the Only Living God and "for in Him we live, and move, and have our being . . ." (Acts 17:28). My position in writing this book is to inform non-Christians and Christians about how my best friend *Jesus Christ* held, comforted, encouraged, empowered and kept me of sound mind while traveling through this tedious journey.

In writing this book, it is my living testimony that God can and will make the impossible (to man) possible. My confession is that regardless of who you are, your status, your finances, your shadowy past, if you accept Jesus Christ as your Personal Savior (Romans 10:9), be baptized, live and exhibit Him in your life, and continue to serve Him daily, He will never leave or forsake you (Hebrews 13:5). As a Christian, my challenged to each reader (if you haven't accepted Jesus) is to make Jesus Christ the Lord and Savior of your life and experience the best friend you will ever know. Jesus is a friend that will cleave closer to you then a brother (Proverbs 18:24).

It is my attestation that in being obedient to God, He granted me (a sinner saved by grace) numerous desires of my heart (Matthew 6:33) with the inclusion that my desires be in His permissive will. My affirmation while on this tedious journey was learning to depend solely on God regardless of circumstances or predicaments' for He will supply your needs, the Word states, ". . . yet have I not seen the righteous forsaken, nor his seed begging bread . . ." (Psalms 37: 25). While continuing in fervent prayer, striving to do His will (to the best of my ability), by the *Grace and Mercy of God, I made it*.

Background

Growing up in Detroit, Michigan for the most part was changeling even as a child. Ruminating as an adolescent my desire was to become a registered nurse (RN). For some unknown reason (at an early age) my belief was strong in sentiment that this profession was chosen, destined, and conditioned for me. Often emulating a nurse as young as age nine, countless injuries were sustained and nursed back to health without my mother's knowledge. The belief of this dream (or premonition) was often voiced by my mother while she spoke with her friends and family (what an encouragement) members. Nevertheless, reared up in a family of eleven siblings caused this desire to appear unlikely. Even so, my focus did not linger on what my family did not have, but on what my parents instilled in me (*God will provide*).

My order within siblings (six boys and six girls) is the *seventh child* born in the *seventh month, and* on the *seventh day* (often teased by other adolescents as being a bad omen). Diminutive in knowledge at that time, thoughts pondered if there was truth in this daunting indictment until reading passages in the Holy Bible related to the number *seven*. Some significant findings included *spiritual perfection and completion*; God's creation of seven days in a week (Genesis 1 - 2:2), the Sabbath recognized on the seventh-day (Exodus 20, 8:11), and prophecy as defined in the book of Revelation chapters 1 and 8; seven churches, seven spirits, candlesticks, seals, and trumpets. Incidentally, the world views the number seven as being lucky! In my honest opinion, luck had nothing to do with my escalation through endeavors, for luck runs out. Without a doubt, it was God's *Grace and Mercy* that allowed me to sustain.

Growing up as a Pastor's Kid or preacher's kid (PK), enthusiasm evolved concerning the Word of God. One would often find me at the feet of my father (very spiritually inclined) inquiring about the Kingdom of God, God's Word, and what was needed to enter into

Heaven. Unexpectedly being filled with the Holy Spirit at the age of five, perception prompted me in to believing my path from that point on would be effortless and painlessly (little was known what was in store for me). It's mystifying how my brain does not remember some current events but remembers this particular event as if it happened yesterday.

While in the choir stand (on the front role) leading a song (*I'm a Soldier in the Army of the Lord*) my voice (in the midst of the song) became speechless. My entire body became very warm and fear followed. After reaching over the banister in front of me and grabbing my mother (she was playing the piano) for safety, the fear became greater and this potential remedy was to no avail, for she began to shout and scream very loudly which scared me even more.

Now running and grabbing my father (standing at the pulpit podium) and holding onto him with a dear life hug, my mind became even more baffled after seeing copious tears run down his face. This scene was very unusual in seeing my father cry. After holding my father for a few minutes he humbly led me back to my seat in the choir stand; but at that time, many members in the congregation were shouting and crying. All of the howling and crying caused me to cry due to panic and not knowing what was happening. Upon arrival home and summoning my father as to what had happened, he informed me the Holy Spirit was upon me (Praise God).

Statement of the Uncertainty
    Being reared as a PK was ambiguous in nature. The mandates of going to church and learning about God was enjoyable, but why so often for PK's? Attendance was required at Wednesday night Bible class, Friday night prayer services, Saturday night choir rehearsals, and Sunday services which included: Sunday school, morning and evening services. Being inquisitive, the question was asked of my parents if all of this time spent in church was necessary. Not surprisingly, as spoken by my father, "As for me in my house we will serve the Lord" (Joshua 24:15). Soon this task would be challenging while feeling very different in relationship to other children my age who did not attend church. For the most part, being a PK one was mainly allowed to affiliate with other children who were on the same spiritual pathway.
    Nevertheless, my childhood was productive and blissful while learning multiple roles in church etiquettes: secretary, Sunday school teacher, devotion leader, interim trustee, prayer leader, and choir member. The thought of expediently growing up and leaving home to do as one pleases (specifically not going to church as frequent as required by my parents) dominated my mind. My yearning was to do as other children (my age) in my environment such as, going to parties (although some parties were allowed), hanging out late (after the street lights had gone off), going to sleepovers, and sleeping in on some Sundays. However, my zeal in reading Biblical materials continued. Glancing back, surprisingly my intellect

never questioned my parent's mandates on attending school five days a week and my nerve of becoming angry when school was missed (even when ill) was an outrage (*Hum*...). Yet, my parents were questioned by me concerning the mandates of church attendance (forgive me Father).

Soon a lesson would be learned on the significance of being in a church environment which increases ones sustainability and anchorage in Jesus Christ. While adhering to my parents mandates and attending church faithfully, inadvertently my steps slipped off course while trying to fit in with peers. Often ending up in ungodly predicaments, a sense of guiltiness penetrated my soul ultimately leading to prayer and asking God for forgiveness and hopes that my parents would never find out. While God is a forgiving God, my thoughts were, how often and how long would He forgive me? Conversely, this pattern of disobedience continued throughout Junior high school. While feeling guilty concerning my disobedience, contentment was felt concerning my academic achievements which in my mind was the only ticket needed regarding my future plans to become a nurse. My thoughts were, my parents did not know of my disobedience and my mission to become a nurse was on the way and nothing was going to stop me (in for a rude awakening).

CHAPTER 2
RAMIFICATIONS OF DISOBEDIENCE

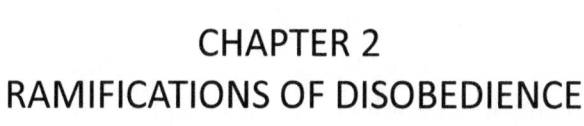

My parents were adamant in teaching one to be obedient and when rules were broken chastisement followed. Often one would hear my parents say obedience is better than sacrifice, although the Bible states this quote a little different in 1st Samuel 15:22, ". . . Behold, to obey is better than sacrifice . . .", nonetheless, intermittently this message was heard and received. What exactly did this mean other than chastisements (called whippings or killings) given by my parents? Well, one would soon find out. After reaching my teenage years and becoming defiant the results led to motherhood at a young age and potential prolongation of my vision to become a nurse.

Even worse, this act of disobedience caused great shame, hurt, and disappointment towards my parents which was non-expunging or recanting. Howbeit, my parents continued to love me and support my educational endeavors. Thank God my mother assisted in caring for my child during the surmising of my High School diploma. Still while feeling lowly concerning the disenchantment reflected on my parents, praises were continually given to God for providing me with parents that never lost faith or hope in me.

Remaining defiant at times, one day my mother ordered me to leave home. Although prompting me to leave, my inner spirit knew she loved and cared for me. Not wanting to leave but remaining obedient, the move took place and my new home was now with a male counterpart. What an awkward situation, feeling uncomfortable being away from home but on the flip side liberty was experienced. Why no contentment with my new arrangements? God knew my heart lingered to be home with my parents and I humbly believe He employed a freak accident that would cause me to return home. Several months away from home while walking up the stairs from the basement my feet tripped and the aftermath was an injured nose. How does anyone trip going up the stairs? Still trying to figure this one out, the outcome would be even more questionable but never forgotten.

After several weeks of experiencing epistaxis (nosebleed) in which several doctors in emergency rooms and outpatient clinics could not control, my body became extremely weak. The bleeding would stop for a while and then return. My nose bled so much five pounds of weight was loss. Becoming mind-puzzled followed by generalized weakness led me to my oldest sister Ann to seek assistance since she was a nurse aide. Upon seeing my swollen nose with large blood clots hanging out of each nostril and my discolored face she immediately stated, *we need to call daddy*.

Immediately, panic and shame suppressed me stemming from the quilt of no longer living at home and now shacking with a male friend. Surly this position was embarrassing to my father (pastor of the church). Even so, my dad was very humble, robust, and steadfast. In addition, he was a loving man, highly respected, and a pastor who loved his children *no matter what*. Many posit my father was blessed with healing powers from God; for many years rumors were heard in regards to my father praying, laying-on-hands, and healing individuals. Erroneous beliefs pondered my mind concerning my father's proclaimed healing powers (yet, there was no doubt in my mind regarding the knowledge of my father being a man of God). Nevertheless, my sister made the call.

The Miracle

My sister Ann led me to the guest bedroom to relax while we waited for dad to arrive. Because of my nosebleed, only an erect position sufficed while sitting on the bed; lying supine was out of the question. The pain generating from my nose prompted me to rock back and forth while breathing through my mouth. Suddenly my father's voice was heard speaking to my sister. As my father entered the room the strangest thing happened; coolness entered in with him. The cool breeze provoked me to murmur under my breath; *what in the world is happening*, but verbally stating only, *hello dad*. My father smiled and asked me what had happened; then he frontward leaned over me and put his right hand on my forehead and started moving it back and forth (from my forehead to the tip of my nose) while asking me this question, *when your problems become too hard for man to solve, who can solve them?* But for some reason my voice was malfunctioning, after several attempts, *Jesus* was forcefully voiced out in a loud tone. Again, *what was that?*

Instantly, after forcing out my Savior's Name *Jesus* . . . breaths of air seeped through my nostrils instead of out of my mouth as before and without delay my feet hit the floor rushing to the bathroom to look at my nose. As God is my witness, *the clots disappeared.* Certainly, I was now a believer of the rumors heard over the years regarding my father's gift of healing, praises of thanks was rendered to God for this healing through my father. Even more miraculous, my nose has not bled from that particular day to present. While grateful of the miracle, fear creped in concerning my current living arrangements which resulted in me packing my bags and returning home without my mother's consent. Too my surprise my mother said nothing but her countenance appeared content in her daughter's return home.

After several years passed the urge to leave home (in the right way) became evident to the point of commitment into an unequally yoked marriage. Surely the Word of God warns us regarding unequally yoked with unbelievers (2nd Corinthians 6:14); yet again disobedient for the mere purpose of leaving home caused despair. This defiant move resulted in a non-supportive relationship in regards to religion and higher education (what a rude awakening). An attempt to sustain my marriage was made by dropping out of a local University; what a deceit (*have mercy Lord*).

Nonetheless, in a short period the marriage was resolved and my engagement in worldly activities (still attending church faithfully) sky-rocketed. Now a single parent with two beautiful daughters there was urgency and a need to become more serious concerning myself and my daughter's future. The decision was made to enroll in a community college to continue my education. But where will a dependable person to care for my children be found? Surely God will provide.

Jesus Still Knocking

While the road was tedious God was gracious (unmerited favor) in allowing me to meet a wonderful caring woman (Mrs. Louise Young: Thank you heavenly Father) while working as a nurse-aide at a local hospital. Mrs. Young enjoyed my presence so much she decided to adopt me as her god-daughter. To my advantage (while dually enrolled in a community college and a medical assistant school), she taught me to sew and offered to tend to my children. One could argue my thirst for knowledge was overdue.

Mrs. Louise Young was the finest babysitter one could retain, she loved and cared for me and my children as if we were her own. Not only did Mrs. Young assist me but her husband Mr. Lonnie Young (now both deceased) was close by her side when care was tendered to my children. While catching the bus to my destinations, faithfully, the Young's picked-up my children regardless of the weather: rain, snow, sleet, hail, etc., (Thank you Father God) they were there. Humbly speaking, Mrs. Young (in my honest opinion) was an angel sent from God to assist me throughout my tedious journey? Respectfully, my belief was that there was nothing in her power she would not do for me (Thank you heavenly Father for putting her in my path).

God was gracious in allowing me to complete medical assistance school, graduate with an Associate Degree in Science from the community college, and gain a decent job as a medical assistant at a local outpatient clinic. Feeling positive concerning my achievements thus far, something tragically happened causing me to feel as if my whole world was coming apart. My father passed and ten months later my mother passed.

Severely distraught, my initial thought was God had turned his back on me and now His wrath was upon me due to my partial submission to Him. Sadden and irate, my hopes and dreams of becoming a nurse (also my mother's dream) appeared insignificant. After all, my mother would not be here to see this accomplishment. And what about my plans to bestow her with the many gifts she so desired and deserved? In making matters worse, her passing was just before mother's day.

Horrified, an attempt was to question the unquestionable God, knowing no one has a right. For the word of God states, "What right does the clay have to question the potter? (Romans 9:20-21)." Suddenly, a soothing hymn came to mind which was often sung by my mother who was gifted by God with multiple gifts: pianist, organist, writer of poems/songs, beautician, seamstress, excellent cook, interior and exterior decorator, gardener, and soloist. My mother's voice bared resemblance to the powerful alto singer Mahalia Jackson, yet my mother sung soprano, alto, tenor, and bass with great emotions and Stella performances that cultivated many. The hymn that came to mind was written by Adelaide A. Pollard in 1907 and is titled *Have Thine Own Way, Lord*. Pollard in 1902, was inspired to write this hymn after being financially unable to travel to Africa to do missionary work. Pollard while feeling considerably dispirited and attending prayer services was approached by an aged woman who inspired her after speaking these words, "It really doesn't matter what you do with us, Lord, just have your own way with our lives." Missionary Pollard that very night wrote this hymn stemming from Jeremiah 18:3 (Wikipedia, 2012).

Two of my favorite verses are:

> ♪ *"Have Thine own way, Lord! Have Thine own way!*
> *Thou art the Potter, I am the clay.*
> *Mold me and make me after Thy will,*
> *While I am waiting, yielded and still.*

♪ *Have Thine own way, Lord! Have Thine own way!*
Wounded and weary, help me, I pray!
Power, all power, surely is Thine!
Touch me and heal me, Savior divine."
(The Blue Book, n.d.)

Nonetheless, questions weighed heavy on my weary mind. Why did this happen, did not God know my need for loving, cherishing, and belonging to my parents? No longer able to call or visit my parents (especially my mother); *help me Jesus* . . . was unimaginable. Knowing God provide answers when one waits patiently (Romans 8:24-25) my heart was burdened and my sole needed answers that very moment.

The heartache felt during this time was so great there was no desire to deal with anything and led to *unintentional regards* for others and my children. Sliding beyond despair, help was needed from God to comfort my weary soul. God said that He will be a comforter for those suffering (2nd Corinthians 1:3-7); yet, no relief was felt for a long period of time. In fact, generalized weakness, weight loss, and the will to live begin to consume me.

What must I do? Had God cursed me for being disobedient and now the repercussions were in progress? The word of Gods states in Deuteronomy 11:26-28, "Behold, I set before you this day a blessing and a curse; A blessing, if ye obey the commandments of the LORD your God, which I command you this day: And a curse, if ye will not obey the commandments of the LORD your God, but turn aside out of the way which I command you this day, to go after other gods, which ye have not known." Was it possible to be blessed and cursed simultaneously? The acceptance of Jesus Christ as my Savior began as a youth, yet straddling the fence continued. Now it was time to sincerely repent, and at that moment the voice of my father echoed inwardly saying, *trust in the Lord*.

    My prayers begin silently asking God to help me, strengthen me, and forgive me for being disobedient and questioning His will. Deep down inside it was a known fact the deaths of my parents was God's Will. In addition, the Bible forewarns us that ". . . it is appointed unto men once to die . . ." (Hebrews 9:27), but how many of us are prepared in facing the death of love one(s)? The passing of my parents took toil and placed emptiness on the inside in which no one *but Jesus* could fill. Spiritually knowing, God handle situations in His time span and in ways that are not necessary our ways (Isaiah 55:9; Romans 8:28), my need from this despair (in my mind) warranted immediate relief.

    Surprisingly, my relief would stem from adversity with my male companion who appealed to me (reverse psychology; so he states) stating my stance and reactions at this particular time was self-centered without consideration of my children. Wow, how dare this man state such things and suppose to love me? Did he not see my state of grieving? What happen to showing compassion and comforting your brothers and sisters (2nd Corinthians 1:3-7) or lamenting with those who are mourning? (Romans 12:15).

Well, the dispute escalated and after much disagreement (have mercy Lord) regarding this disposition an explicit self-examination evolved. My God, he was right; consideration of my children was unthought-of while waddling in self-pity over the grief of my parents (mom's guilt). While continuing in prayer, my energy levels and the will to live return (Thank you Lord). Much comfort and strength was gained by reading my Bible, especially after learning that suffering causes one to be obedient. Hebrews 5:7-8, states, " Who in the days of his flesh, when he had offered up prayers and supplications with strong crying and tears unto him that was able to save him from death, and was heard in that he feared. Though he were a Son, *yet learned he obedience* by the things which he suffered."

On a much lighter note, moving forward was important while praying strongly for God to strengthen and carry me through this grievous period (as always, God calmed and continues to comfort me), thank you Jesus! After reasonable healing, an attempt was made to enter into nursing school with no avail. Basically, the dean of nursing informed me of not qualifying (even after completing 2.5 years of prerequisites) at this community college. Truthfully, this reply was inconceivable, for all necessary requirements (even my grades) for the registered nurse (RN) program were suffice.

Initially, my self-worth and hopes were low in accomplishing my dream of becoming a nurse all because of the dean of nursing' summation. In fact, upon completion with the dean, the thought of not being *nursing material* clouded my mind and potentiated choosing another profession. Truly, one should never allow anyone to intimidate them, for God will always be on your side and "We are more than conquerors through him that loved us" (Romans 8:37). Reflecting back on the song, *I am a Solider in the Army of the Lord were my thoughts* and regardless of what the dean stated my God is the ultimate judge over inconclusive verdicts. Deep down inside being a nurse was my lifetime dream which initiated seeking other avenues in making this dream come true.

God led me to contact a dear friend by the name of Marie Shoulders (already a license practical nurse (LPN) who encouraged me (from that day to this one) concerning my dream of becoming a nurse. Marie informed me about the LPN program she previously attended and to my advantage God blessed me in passing the entrance exam and being accepted with all expenses paid by the state (Praise the Lord). Expenses included tuition, uniforms, books, and forty dollars per week for miscellaneous items. While the program was a blessing, arriving back and forth was challenging and often funding was low in trying to get to and from my destination in addition to purchasing lunch (after being in school all day) but God was merciful.

One time in particular (not having bus fare) God was petitioned to allow me to get on the bus without a problem (only had a small amount of change). My hope was that after making it to school one of my friends would loan me money to return home. As God is my witness, the change was thrown in the fare box while proceeding to the back of the bus. The bus driver gazed at me in dismay but said nothing (Thank you Lord). No doubt God was looking out for me . . . yes, He looked beyond my faults and saw my needs (Thank you Heavenly Father). Often my friends would buy or share their lunch with me and sometimes my belief was that God miraculously filled my aching empty stomach with the aromas of the food (Praise the Lord) stemming from the school's cafeteria.

Looking back, God has truly blessed me while travelling on this journey as my body was: drenched in rain storms, freezing in snow storms, and scorched by the sun during heat waves while waiting at bus stops. Nevertheless, this endeavor was completed with high honors and my title was now a graduate License Practical Nurse. While many voiced my completion of this program would never happen, God proved the contrary; one person in particular was a nursing instructor. This particular instructor had an irreligious spirit and would always emphasize my destiny as *ending up on John C. Lodge;* whatever that meant. Howbeit, praises are due to the Lord for his encouraging Words, "The Lord is my light and my salvation; whom shall I fear? The Lord is the strength of my life; of whom shall I be afraid? When the wicked, even mine enemies and my foes came upon me to eat up my flesh, they stumbled and fell" (Psalms 27:1-3).

Indisputably, when God have a blessing for you, no one can curse you. For "God is not a man, that he should lie; neither the son of man, that he should repent: hath he said, and shall he not do it? Or hath he spoken, and shall he not make it good? Behold, I have received commandment to bless: and he hath blessed; and I cannot reverse it" (Numbers 23:19-20). One must never let anyone destroy your dreams! When individuals are not for you, they are against you. Move forward and "Let this mind be in you, which was also in Christ Jesus . . ." (Philippians 2:5) and God will keep you in perfect peace when your mind is focused on him (Isaiah 26:3). Unfortunately, in this life one will encounter naysayers but must remain focused on the tasks at hand. Still, God will place positive individuals in your path as with me (praise Him). Some instructors took me under their wings to ascertain my best foot was put forward while completing tasks. Although some were stern and vigorous, reverence is given to God for them and my parents whom all enhanced my humbleness, perseverance, and temperance spirit.

Accomplishing the LPN credentials was a milestone and one of the happiest days of my life. The mere fact that God brought me through this wearisome task (although non-deserving) was just awesome. Although my mother was not present in the flesh, spiritually I could hear her voice saying, *that's my daughter she is a nurse.* God blessed me by allowing my oldest sister (Ann) to stand in my mother's stead in seeing me become a nurse: for my sister Ann always treated me as a daughter and not a sister. In agreement with the Bible, unwavering faith and persevering through trials and tribulations makes one stronger and fit for God's usage. According to 1st Peter 1:7, "... the trial of your faith, being much more precious than of gold that perisheth, though it be tried with fire, might be found unto praise and honour and glory at the appearing of Jesus Christ."

Upon passing the State's Board Examination (another milestone, Thank you Lord) and receiving my LPN license to practice, my first job as a nurse (local hospital) was gained resulting in making decent money to support my children more efficiently. Excitingly, a call was made to my friend Marie, now a Registered Nurse (RN) to inform her of my achievements. After graciously congratulating me she proceeded with urgency for me to pursue my RN status. In an attempt to inform her that she was fanatical and of my exaltations from the LPN program, Marie not only gave me a miniature sermon on the importance of returning to RN school but revealed significant incentives for returning. Affirmation was given to my friend on future returning to school and after working alone side my fellow co-workers (RN's) it was confirmed that my return was imperative. Marie was right, for my desire was to be a RN from the beginning. Nevertheless, at this time celebrating my LPN victory and glorifying God for this achievement was forefront.

But, "What shall I render unto the Lord for all his benefits toward me?" (Psalms 116:12), spiritually knowing that even my best effort would not be good enough while still worldly partying and attending church faithfully. Yet, Jesus was still knocking. Jesus declares in Revelation 3:20, "Behold, I stand at the door, and knock: if any man hear my voice, and open the door, I will come in to him, and will sup with him, and he with me." While knowing that straddling-the fence- was wrong and displeasing to God, my weaken flesh continued to thrive against His will. My soul constantly felt guilty while instantly being reminded from a soft inward voice stating, "So then because thou art lukewarm, and neither cold nor hot, I will spue thee out of my mouth" (Revelations 3:16). Still, disobedience to God continued.

Without a doubt, my spirit felt Jesus knocking at the door of my heart but surrendering totally to him was not idea since my partying continued and from my perspective, the night life was as much enjoyable as attending church services. Indeed, attending cabarets, enjoying entertainment such as bands, dancers, singers, and comedians overly excited and thrilled me. More excitedly, was seeing several of my brothers (Mark and Jonathan who had started a dance group) perform at various events. In my humble opinion, Mark was such an extravagant dancer that even MC Hammer or Usher didn't stand a chance competing against him. Imprudently thinking, the night life was the right life and New Year's Eve was my major night of worldly partying. Often while attending church *Watch Night* services on New Years' Eve one could ascertain my partying clothes were packed for an expedient change and then proceeding to a New Years' Eve party. Foolishly, my beliefs were that in the midst of my wrong doings and infirmities God would always be there for me . . ., at least my bed at this time was undefiled (now married again).

After a year of working as a LPN, again my heart was grief stricken due to the demise of my oldest brother: Willie Thomas Jr. Once more, God carried me through this grieving process. Even so, my schedule was busier than ever with church, work (now two years as a LPN), partying, and now enrolled in a RN program at a community college. Still, Jesus loved me in spite of my faults. One weekend after working relentlessly at church, no strength was left to study for an important pharmacology exam the upcoming Monday. Feeling nervous concerning this exam my heavenly Father was petitioned for strength and mercy to at least pass this exam (75% was needed). While strongly believing that God would have mercy on me in regards to this exam, He did. In fact, God showed up and showed out (Thank you Jesus).

To my surprise, upon corrections' of the exams the instructor announced how she was very disappointed in outcome of the low test scores (now shaking like a leaf on a tree during a strong breeze). She went on to say, how very pleased she was with one student's (approximately 30 students in the class) significant outcome of scoring 100% on the exam; *and that student was me*. Now really *shaking in my boots*, after reviewing the exam and validating the instructor's findings, my humble spirit felt that God Himself had taken the exam. This revelation is not to be taken as being cynical or boasting but as graciousness in giving God praises and glory. After thanking God from the bottom of my heart provisions were made in allotting time to study for future exams.

Nursing school was very challenging and required great sacrifices in completion of this endeavor. Often instructors posit that while in nursing school students must be married to their books; this statement is not far from the truth even when one puts God first. Fact: God should always come first. Using logic, my thoughts were, if God was with me while straddling the fence, how much more will He be with me upon fully committing to Him? After resolving my second failed marriage a vow was made to be fully committed and obedient to my one and only true God. In addition, my petition to God was that if He would bring me through the RN program my commitment and services will forever be imparted to Him.

God became busier than ever in making a way for me. God blessed me in meeting another individual who played a significant role in my life and endeavors by the name of (Lynda Dolphus). Lynda has been a close friend from the time we met to this present day. Lynda's mother Ms. Shirley (another blessing, she often picked me up when we attended LPN school) introduced us. Recently (June-2013) after speaking with Ms. Shirley (they both visited my church) she informed me that she knew my father and he baptized her when she attended his church on 12th Street. How outstanding to hear (after all these years) that Ms. Shirley knew and met my father at the very church in which my soul encountered the Holy Ghost. Again, God was in the plan and was now working through Shirley's daughter Lynda. Throughout my nursing careers (RN,

BSN, and Masters in Nursing) Lynda greatly assisted me and has played an integral role in my family endeavors. One thing's for sure if no one else cheered me on Lynda was always there saying, *it's going to be alright girlfriend you're almost there*. Not only has Ms. Shirley and Lynda been there for me physically and emotionally, but financially they both supported many of my church's' fundraisers as well. Praise God for my friends Ms. Shirley and Lynda, their kindness will never be forgotten. God always has a plan.

A Guided Blessing

God works in mysterious ways, nearing the completion of my RN program my funds were depleted and financial assistance was needed to complete my final course with a deadline. Numerous resources were sought without prevail and the deadline was fast approaching. In panic, Jesus was petitioned and he led me to my youngest sister (Wanda) who had very little finances at that time. Nevertheless, she was eager to assist me even though she would be late tending to her own affairs. She informed me how important my needs were versus her own affairs (bless her sweet heart) and loaned me the finances without missing a beat. Thank you Jesus . . . was my reply while moving forward (Praise Him).

God blessed and permitted me to graduate as a RN which was another gracious milestone (unworthy of). For God allowed me to complete nursing school, yet my pledge to serve him diligently after completion was not fulfilled. As reminded in Matthew 21:12 that,

"God is a rewarder of those that diligently seek him", but why the favor in me? Nevertheless, as taught from youth serving diligently in church continued, the same holds for still straddling the fence (Thank you Lord for being longsuffering and forgiving). The aftermath of my disobedience ultimately resulted in two failed marriages, again shacking with a male acquaintance, and now three wonderful daughters (have mercy Lord). Thank God, in spite of my disobedience he continued to love, watch over me and my children while keeping us out of harm's way. Nonetheless, convictions were imminent.

Dr. Juanita Crawford
-Ed.D, MSN, RN-

ASA Publishing Corporation

CHAPTER 3
IMPLICATIONS OF BEING OBEDIENT

Overtime, the Spirit of God convicted me concerning going to worldly events. The conviction in itself was amazing; for my intentions was never to give up the night life. Yet, my perceptions of the night life as having a high-quality time soon came to an end. The convictions became stronger and stronger resulting in actual sympathy for individuals encountered while being out in the night life environment. Desires to dance, consume alcohol (as often consumed at that time), and mingle dissipated.

Questions evolved in my mind while attending night life events such as, how many people in this environment knew Jesus and how many had no desire to know or accept Him as their personal Savior. Then the ultimate questions concerning myself evolved, what would happen to me if Christ returned at this very hour and found me in this type of setting, or what if my demised occurred in this type of setting and where will my destiny be spent? Would God forgive me although

His righteous ways were known but not adhered too? Convictions concerning my shacking-up followed and resulted in me moving out.

A reflection of this scripture crossed my mind while being convicted, "and that servant, which knew his lord's will, and prepared not himself, neither did according to his will, shall be beaten with many stripes" (Luke 12:47). *Beaten, have mercy Lord, please no Lord not me,* was my reply! For, anyone touching me (in a defensive way) for the most part has never been condoned. Truly, deep down inside my spirit was quenched concerning my disobedience to God while remembering how my Savior continued to love, watch over, provide, and care for me and my children, in spite of my faults. Truly, this was the time to fully commit myself to God.

Fully Committed

Fervently praying, God was called upon and asked to deliver, strengthen, guide, and help me to become a beacon of light in relationship to drawing others to Him. All the same, many so-called-friends were loss due to my repentance. Yet, the most awesome friend of all; Jesus was gained. My most prominent words became *Lord, have mercy on me.* Yes, my soul was in need of a spiritual overhaul. Although church attendance was adhered to since birth, it wasn't until my late thirties my spirit humbly surrendered to my Lord and Savior Jesus Christ. Thank you God *Jehovah Mekadesh* (Sanctify; set apart or separate; Leviticus 20:8).

Now the worth and philosophy of my parents in training-up the child in the way that they should go (Proverbs 22:6) was known. Revisiting my childhood upbringing concerning the Lord and the house of God (Church) my heart now inherently engaged and enjoyed attending church services. My parents taught us (the children) to always partake in church services and never be a bench warmer and often voiced, *there is always work to do in the house of the Lord*. One version of the Bible Matthew 20:4 denotes, "You also go and work in my vineyard, and I will pay you whatever is right" (New International Version).

My roles in the church were multiple: choir member, willing worker, the nurse's guild, and a primary class Sunday school teacher. While working on various auxiliaries, a significant principle was now understood; *people are a product of their environment* (voiced by elderly individuals during my youth) *many come and many go*. Humbly speaking, retention as a devout Christian involves steadfast in a Christian environment, fervently praying and asking for forgiveness and strength, dedication as a parishioner; constantly reading and engulfing the word of God, and exemplifying a Christian in one's everyday walk. Besides, what good am I without my God, who can supply all of my needs and desires of my heart?

Desires of my Heart

Again married and now a devout Christian a desire to continue my education (obtaining a Bachelor, Master, and Doctoral Degree) weighed heavy on my heart and mind. In addition to obtaining secular degrees other desires included: living to see my children grow up, become married, graduate from college, give birth to their children, and also to partake in making a gospel compact disc (CD). Praise God, by His Grace and *Mercy* my Faith had increased to the extent that anything could be accomplished through Christ. Bless *Jehovah Rohi* (The Lord is my Shepherd; I shall not want . . . Psalm 23:1).

Spiritually and logically thinking, my precious Savior was with me and my family thus far (even while straddling the fence), surly He would be with me now that I was fully committed. God was so gracious in assisting me to settle down and He blessed me to become a 2nd time home owner. So without hesitantly (and no secured tuition) a bachelor degree in nursing was pursued and accomplished (joy bells are ringing in my soul). Appreciative of this degree being completed was an understatement, for this course was very demanding and even required class attendance on Independence Day. God had mercy on me while completing this significant milestone, for my schedule was very hectic: working full-time, taking care of home and family, highly dedicated to my church activities, and I was also singing in a gospel group with my cousins, praise Him, *Jehovah Shammah* (The Lord is there; Ezekiel 48:35).

In the midst of God showering me with his unmerited favor my mind dwelled on my two older daughters (Kimberly; better known as Kimbo) and (Franita; better known as Punkin) and my desires for them to enroll and graduate from college. Often my daughters would inform me they were going to enroll in college however; this process had yet to occur; so my prayers and hopes continued. My youngest daughter (Ronda: better known as Precious) was attending junior high school and was doing well. Eager for more nursing knowledge enrollment in the Master's of Nursing program took place while still overwhelmed and excited about completing the bachelor's program. Exhausted at times was an understatement, nonetheless, prayers for strength continued, for all endeavors were enjoyed (with exception of accruing student loans). Still, one is blessed in qualifying for loans/scholarships and my belief is that God has plans for my debt resolutions (bless you Lord).

Nevertheless, another financial issue aroused. Due to mass number of typed assignments required in the master's program a computer was necessary. Now my fear of computers would be faced while learning to become computer savvy. Fortunately and blessed, throughout the bachelor's program (after writing my assignments) my wonderful niece Delvata Roberta Evans typed and printed out my assignments (bless you dear niece). Because of time constraints and increasing assignments (one due the first day of class) the need for a home computer and printer was eminent. A trip was made to a nearby electronic store with my niece Dawnita Trudane Woods after praying to God to allow me to qualify for a computer and printer. Pleading: Lord help me, for no clue was known as to what kind of computer and printer to purchase upon credit approval.

After submitting the application the sales representative returned shortly and informed me of the approval (yes, praising God on the inside); he then humbly assisted in selecting an appropriate computer and printer. Thank you God, my prayers were answered and now the challenge of pursuing my master's degree in nursing was on the way. While nearing the end of the master' program God blessed our gospel group in completing our CD, praise my Lord *El Shaddai* (Almighty God; Genesis 17:1). How exciting this was to have two accomplishments in one year (Glory be to God). Inconceivably, these challenges were mind-boggling and tedious, yet God blessed and planted various individuals in my path to assist with these completions. Not only was the our group's CD completed, but because the executive producer favored my awesome singing cousin Carolyn Jacobs, we accrued no remuneration for the production or distributions of our CD (bless you Dr. E. LaQuint Weaver; Producer and my cousin Rev. Frank Jerai Knolton; group Manager) for your hard work. Great honor is due to my Lord, *El Elyon* (God Most High; Genesis 14:19-20).

A year after completing my Master's Degree, my oldest sister (Ann) passed. Again, feelings of distraught and alienation consumed my sole, for my sister Ann had taken on my mother's stead and always made provisions to assist, encourage, talk, and comfort me. Humbly and often my sister gave and loaned me money; honestly my spirit at times felt she had given me her last dime. Sometimes she would show up at my church (unannounced) to check up on me; this act really touched my heart. My sister although slim in stature did not back down from anyone and no one dared to mess with me (in any form or fashion) once they found out Ann was my sister. Ann would state, *I will kill a brick*. In addition to my parents, my sister Ann was highly appreciated for voicing a great deal of confidence in me. Ann like my mother had such a beautiful voice (sung like an angel). In fact, my entire family has been blessed with a singing ministry. My second oldest sister Gwendolyn has a glorious voice (in my honest opinion) which is a high pitch soprano that sounds like a bird. My brother Rev. David Ford voice reminds me of my favorite late rhythm and blues (R&B) singer Luther Vandross. Between my mother and Ann, our family (specifically, the girls) were often singing on someone's church program. Again, God stepped right in and carried me through the demise of my sister; she was a blessing to me. My mother, my sister Ann, and my godmother Mrs. Louise Young always instructed and encouraged me to continue with my education to the highest level to the best of my ability, and now my dual enrollment in two Universities took place in pursuit of my graduate certificate in nursing education and my doctor of education degree.

My plans were now to prepare to teach in the nursing arena. Becoming a nursing professor was the ultimate desire of my heart which developed while in RN school; however, no immediate plans were contemplated. Ruminating back on my last nursing course (transitions) while pursuing my RN degree my

Professor (doctoral level) gave the class an assignment which consisted of writing a five-year plus future plans. While presenting, my future vows (boldly stated) were to obtain my bachelors, masters, doctoral degree, and eventually become a nursing professor. Praise God, my vows were almost completed yet, for some unknown reason my spirit remained introverted and extremely nervous at the very thought of standing in front of a classroom.

Truthfully, my comfort zone is being behind the scenes; nevertheless, others tend to nominate or delegate me (especially my mother mandating I lead songs and recite poems and readings) to be on the front scene. Yet, the desire to teach was still at hand and the decision to enroll in a doctoral program in preparation of becoming effective in my teaching methods was made. Inwardly thinking, was this just an excuse to put off teaching at the moment? For one only needed a bachelor degree to begin teaching. Nevertheless, this request was taken to the altar as a desire of the heart and for God to order my steps. Undoubtedly, God knows me better than myself and His plans for me are the pre-eminent plans. In concurrence, Jeremiah 29:11 states, "For He cares for me and my future and destiny lies in His hands."

By no means known, God was working (in my mind) expeditiously regarding this matter behind the scenes. While attending the local University in pursuit of a post graduate certificate in nursing education my nursing professor asked the ultimate question of the class (all established master's prepared nursing students); *who all are now nursing instructors?* All (exempting myself) raised their hands. This professor while firm and bold was very instructive, pleasant, intelligent, and for some reason strongly favored me. Although all students were treated with kindness and respect, a stronger compassion lingered in regards to me. She would always encourage and give me complements concerning my completed coursework and future educational endeavors.

Her favor extended to the point of writing grants which ultimately caused reversal of students' tuition paid for two courses (only needed three) taken with this professor at this University, thank you my God *Adonai* (Lord; Genesis 15:2). Still, this professor went a step further (appearing firm in statue) and voiced her position on my need to start teaching. Surprised and humbly smiling, this message was written off while feeling inferior as to being the only Master's prepared RN student in the class not teaching (including the younger students). What was unknown to me was this Professor was now working on my behalf behind the scenes. My initiative in trying to find a teaching position consisted of asking several colleagues in relationship to acquiring a nursing teaching position; their responses were, *one needed to have at least two years of teaching experience.*

Plausibly thinking; how does one acquire experience if no one hires them? On the other hand, spiritually and meekly murmuring under my breath, *apparently they do not know the God I serve* which can make all things possible. Jesus stated, ". . . With God all things are possible" (Matthew 19:26). Lord and behold, approximately two weeks later a phone call came in from the Dean of Nursing at a community college (later found out this dean was a friend of my professor) asking me to teach a particular class? Of course my reply was yes, and an interview was schedule. Astonished and puzzled, the question surfaced; how could this possibly be? For several applications had been submitted to this particular school in the past yet, no callbacks were received. In addition, some of my colleagues had submitted applications (over the years) without prevail.

Moreover a week later, another call was received from a colleague (befriended in the masters' program) informing me that a nearby university was seeking nursing instructors for their LPN course. Upon inquiring about this position, another interview was scheduled. While praising God for the privilege of being scheduled for the two interviews my body became nervous as a wreck. In the midst of my nervousness a confession of my concerns were voiced to a humble deacon at the church I was currently attending. Truly this nervousness evolved out of fear. Where was this fear coming from? Knowing that "God hath not given us the spirit of fear; but of power, and of love, and of a sound mind" (2nd Timothy 1:7) my mind was bewildered.

This particular deacon was a man of little words but the few words he spoke would never be forgotten. This deacon's words linger with me to this present day, specifically when encountering new challenges that are mind-boggling and stomach twitching. He calmly but courageously stated, *God has already equipped you, just believe.* Triumph, these words were so influential they immediately empowered me. Praise God for putting individuals in my pathway to encourage and empower me. Although on my bending knee praying for the interviews to go well, my spirit remained nervous to the point of almost turning around after reaching the parking lot of one site.

Again praying and asking God for strength and boldness, a soft voice stemming from the inside posed the questioned, *where is your faith?* This voice took me back to a passage in the Bible when Jesus rebuked His disciples stating, "Ye of little faith" (Matthew 8:26). Recap: Jesus and His disciples were sailing across the Sea of Galilee and a great windstorm arose that freighted the disciples while Jesus was asleep in the stern. Interestingly, the disciples had walked with Jesus and first handily witnessed Jesus perform numerous miracles prior to calming the sea such as: turning water into wine at a marriage in Cana (John 2:1-11), healing of a nobleman's' son (John 4: 46-54), exorcism of a man in Capernaum (Mark 1:23-28), remedial of His disciple Peter's mother-in law (Matthew 8:14-15), various healings of the sick (Mark 1:32, Luke 4:40-41, the overwhelming catching of fish (Luke 5:3-10), curing of leprosy (Matthew 8:1-3), healing a centurion's servant (Matthew 8:5-13) and a man with palsy (Luke 5:18-26), straightening out a man's withered hand (Matthew 12: 8-14) and resurrecting a widows' son (Luke 7:11-17).

Still the disciples' faith wavered and they feared

for their lives. Similarly, with status as a devout Christian who confesses Jesus as the head of my life and a self-witness that *nobody but Jesus* brought me through my past trials and tribulations yet, my faith wavers (forgive me Lord). At that moment, Jesus instilled in me the boldness needed to move forward and proceed with the interviews. What's wonderful about Jesus is how He miraculously let you know that He is in the plan and in control by exhibiting something very unusual in nature that one will never forget. Upon interviewing at both sites the interviewers treated me as if they had known me for years and hired me on the spot. God blessed me in teaching at the two colleges (adjunct), while working part-time as a staff nurse, and attending two universities (*God is Awesome*).

One could challenge the moral of this story is three-fold (faith in God, having a spirit of expectancy, and respecting others). First: One must always keep their faith in God , possessing secular degrees are good but not as significant as knowing and reverencing the one who allowed you to accomplish them (thank you Father) and just because one possess a degree does not mean they will automatically gain the job. Second: Gain a spirit of expectancy (the desire to teach), but be careful of what you ask for you if you are not ready to receive it, remember God will give you the desires of your heart. Third: Never treat people unkindly; treat all with respect for you never know where your help will come from.

God works in mysterious ways, sometimes within people (my professor, my colleague, and the deacon), animals, and even immovable objects. Yes, God is powerful, thank you my God *Jehovah Elohim* (Powerful God; Genesis 1:1). Recap: God used his prophet Elisha to retrieve a borrowed iron axe head that had fallen into the Jordan river, miraculously the axe head floated to the top (2nd Kings 6:3-7). God caused a donkey to speak to his rider Balaam a non-Israelite prophet (Numbers 22:28). Who dare not serve and reverence my God? *Jehovah Jireh* (The Lord Provides; Genesis 22:14).

    God is gracious in giving one the desires of their heart but one must be mindful of their asking. Teaching nursing courses is challenging and rewarding; however, not when one is suffering from burn-out. After completion of the post graduate certificate in nursing education one of my teaching positions was dismissed and my schedule now included working two part-time jobs (staff nurse and nursing professor) while attending doctoral school with one year completed. Still overwhelmed, this process continued. Truly my husband (Rev, Emmett Crawford Jr.) understood my desires or just simply thought of me as being unstable (Bless him Lord for being there). Often he joked about me being married to the computer nevertheless, he supported my endeavors.

CHAPTER 4
HAVOC TIMES

While taking pre-requisites for the doctoral program constantly grave stories were heard concerning this degree. Still my desire (eager and determined to persevere) was to obtain this terminal degree. After researching the university literature concerning the doctoral program the literature projected approximately three years for completion and my mind was set on completing the program as set forth. Wake up call, now headed for a colossal disappointment. This degree remained questionable and inconclusive as to the nature of completion, even upon inquiry regarding doctoral school from post-doctoral graduates; reactions were always daunting followed by diminutive responses. Question: what was so horrendous about the doctoral program that hardly any post- doctorate individuals cared to speak on?

Surprisingly, further research denotes only 1% of United States population hold a doctoral degree; this should have been my clue. Interestingly, 2% of United

States population holds professional degrees (degrees earned in medicine, optometry, law, etc.), 5.9% master degrees, and 6.5% associate degrees (Bauman & Graf, 2003). Humbly, my spirit felt God would allow me to accomplish the doctorate degree but I never imagined experiencing an intimidating challenge. This particular degree required online as well as classroom attendance (called residencies) which were held annually in various States.

The University was private and the tuition was costly, as with many doctoral programs. Often asking, was my mind working effectively in enrolling in the program? For it was a known fact neither myself nor my family had the finances to offset the cost of this degree. Already with outstanding student loans and God on my side the decision was made to move forward.

Prospective Change of Heart

The very first class was a nightmare, from sun-up to sun-down one would find me at the computer adhering to challenging assignments and exams in the cohort conference rooms (this would continue for the next three years). Have mercy Lord, this was unbelievable; quitting at this point pondered my head frequently. My first class was so challenging that I informed my professor that I was going to quit related to the great demands. One class included taking multiple examinations while writing copious papers. After receiving a long-distance call from my professor (which included a long pep talk) my spirit were uplifted and her inspirational speech caused me to continue on while remaining mind boggled.

After speaking with other cohorts, congruently we did not know if we were coming or going. Thank God my cohorts shared my feelings and pains. My mind was task orientated and regardless to where my body led me my mind was focused on assignments (current and future) and their completions. My library was now overstocked with books; literally there were no space for more books. In fact, several bookcases had to be purchased (more money) to accompany them. Most books were very expensive and extremely necessary for validation of one's thoughts (no one dared to validate themselves). Yes, a salient point gained from doctoral school is that no matter how much one knows concerning a subject, without other scholars agreeing (published scholars/peer reviewed authors) with your topic statement(s) or conversation one submission was considered insignificant.

In essence, if one was not a researcher one would soon become one while remaining on this path. Even the terminology of this elite program became challenging to the point that my common spelling and certainly the English language became questionable. For the most part, the doctoral language resembles the language of lawyers and researchers and is now a part of my repertoire. Nonetheless, due to this language change many labeled me as *thinking myself to be better than others*. Foolishness, why would one fault someone for enhancing their skills and train of thoughts? While my speech generally included medical terminology it now congruently employs both medical and law terminology. Enhancements are always good, right? So why would anyone fault another for gaining knowledge? My philosophy is the more knowledge one gains the more knowledge one can share with others.

Nevertheless, acquiring any certificates or degrees from any school or college comes with great sacrifice (specifically, at the doctoral level). Sacrifices include but are not limited to: faith, dedication, commitment, perseverance, and finances. As one moves to a higher educational level higher expectations are required. In fact, our cohort was informed by one professor in regards to the strenuous requirements of the program after we complained about the intensity of the program; his reply was, if *it was easy, anyone would have one.*

The intensity of courses and multiple assignments soon led to a reduction in my usual visits (including phone calls) to family and friends (thank God for those who understood). Nevertheless, time was allocated for holidays (love to eat) and being an excellent cook much was required on my behalf in the kitchen. Some of my holidays specialties are: chitterlings, collard greens with fatback (salt pork), macaroni and cheese, turkey and dressing, and of course my requested homemade sweet potatoes pies. Funny, my brother (Rev. David Ford) would challenge me on my sweet potatoes pies (both included our mother's recipe). My brother's pies are excellent but my sweet potatoes pies are stellar; just kidding, but they are very much so eatable and demanded!

Thank God my mother (an excellent cook) taught all the children who were of the adequate age to cook. My brother Deacon Cornelius Ford could prepare an outstanding meal and sometimes had dinner prepared for the entire family following Sunday morning church services. Yes, we are a family that can put away some food, and often my father would state (while the family was gathered around the dinner table after the blessing), *these are the people that loves to eat*. While joyous, the holidays were short lived and classes soon resumed. After several classes the protocol called for an out of town visit to my first residency. What astronomical figures (appearing faint) were my thoughts after viewing the cost of the residency class and transportation?

Keeping the Faith

Knowing my finances were low a call was made to my sister (Rebecca) regarding my desire to attend the residency. While not expecting a speech as an outcome of our conversation her words were heartwarming, faith enlightening, thought provoking, and never to be forgotten. My sister stated, you are a very good person Juanita and a good Christian, and if God intends for you to go to this residency He will make a way for you. While this response was not anticipated, my overall thoughts were; she is right. Immediately, my faith increased and after ending the call my luggage was packed (now feeling like a millionaire) without concerns of finances.

Surprisingly, several days after talking to my

sister, my husband informed me that his brother (Ricardo) would loan us the finances (my hero, thank you so much dear brother-in-law). This favor imparted to me and my husband from my brother-in-law will never be forgotten. Immediately God was petitioned and given prayers of thanksgiving for his unmerited favor and blessings in allowing me to attend the first residency. For the University had already informed the cohorts that the first residency was mandatory and if unable to attend one would be terminated from the program and would have to be readmitted.

God also blessed me in allowing a member at church (attended at that time) to commit to driving me to and from the designated State of my residency. In addition, my sister (Evangelist Theresa Skinner) also accompanied me to this residency (although no time was allotted in mingling with them due to my exigent schedule). In fact, one day of this residency was centered on my birthday and surprisingly my sister (Rebecca) sent me a beautiful card with a financial blessing enclosed (God is good!). Although the amalgamation of assignments was tedious and challenging all doctoral cohorts were treated as royalty (staff, food, service) while attending the residencies, and the hotel was elegant (*five star*) and suitable for a king. Although we ate well the assignments were non-ending and difficult.

CHAPTER 5
HOLDING ON

Regressing back, the doctoral program was the most challenging task I ever encountered. For the most part, there were frequent oral presentations (group wise and individuals), as well as group and individual writhen assignments. In addition, one was required to continuously compose and respond to various colleagues in the cohort and facilitators' posts on strategic and often assertive subjects in discussion boards. One barely had time to spend with family and friends; therefore frequent family gatherings and vacations were obliterated and occasional family gatherings attended was often accompanied with my laptop and books. Often it appeared many had forsaken and despised my endeavors, nevertheless God was there.

Ignoring Naysayers
Sometimes while attending events mumbling was heard concerning my educational endeavors such

as, *she have been in school all her life*, again, this was not far from the truth. Nevertheless, one could argue that regardless of what one does rather positive or negative there will be naysayers. Truthfully, my purpose of staying matriculated was for gaining knowledge, not because of my fondness for school. In fact, my true two overwhelming favorite subjects are Biblical and nursing knowledge. Some of my greatest Biblical educational challenges and learning stemmed from participating in the Bible Institute while attending my brother's Rev. Demetrius Ford, Psy.D, J.D., Ph.D. church. Humbly speaking, my hard work in studying the Bible and partaking in the Bible Institute at Dayspring Baptist Church paid off and resulted in me being name *Valedictorian* for four years in a row (1996-1999). Praise the Lord, reading Biblical literature (especially the Bible) and attentively listening to biblical leaders, teachers, and speakers greatly inspires me. Often while reading the Word of God my spirit is uplifted resulting in excitement and strengthening of my soul. Amazingly, in reading the Bible, no matter how many times, each time God enlightens one's perspective regarding the scriptures passages (Respectively, Amen).

Nursing within itself (in my honest opinion) is an honorable profession and a humble prudent nurse is a gift from God. Commonalities underlying the two subjects are God's holistic, mysterious, miraculous, and comprehensive works concerning the human body (spiritually, physically, emotionally, and psychologically). Not surprisingly, in proactively protecting the physical as well as spiritual body,

Christians must put on the whole armor of God (Ephesians 6:11-18) to be able to stand against all forces of darkness. In my case, the armor warranted restoration or perhaps needed to be assessed by God.

God Sometimes Challenge Us

Now pursuing the doctorate degree in education my spiritual, mental, and physical wellbeing would now be assessed. God even challenged my employment of the fruit of the spirit while enduring this task. "But the fruit of the Spirit is love, joy, peace, longsuffering, gentleness, goodness, faith; meekness, temperance: against such there is no law" (Galatians 5:22-23). While the fruit of the spirit is eloquently displayed in the Bible, the act of perpetuating them can be challenging especially when one is provoked to anger. Only God can control ones' persona and reactions in the mist of being provoked. Sometimes one has to remain silence in exploiting knowledge even though they have the validity to support their defense. As students while attending classes, one learns that effective knowledge and understanding is gained by remaining silent (until it's time to speak), open, reachable, and teachable. The successful learner never deems themselves as all-knowing. Only God is Omniscience (all knowing) which is his nature (Ps 139:1-6, 13-16).

The sternness of the doctoral program teaches one to become humble, a conscientious listener, self-restraint, and most importantly tolerance. Even when voicing ones opinions and concerns, the outcomes appeared bleak when challenging ones leaders. God in humbling my spirit caused me to become patience while remaining silence which assisted in my escalation through this program (one must remain humble and satisfied with the knowledge God embeds in them). Not surprisingly, God was preparing me for the oral defense (time to speak) and triumph me through. God loves a humble spirit. "Not that we are sufficient of ourselves to think anything as of ourselves; but our sufficiency is of God" (2nd Corinthians 3:5).

God always has a plan for one's life when we are humble, but we must learn to listen to anyone He sends in our paths. One should never limit themselves to thinking that knowledge stems only from individuals with degrees or with high-flying ranks. God is Omnipotence (all powerful) nature of God (John 1:1-5) and he instills knowledge in people of all statues: great or small, young or old, rich or poor, and with or without degrees. In fact, some of my greatest Biblical teachers (without secular degrees) effectively and exegeses disseminated various biblical subject matters (and secular subjects) just as well as some theologians (and sometimes better). Incidentally, many salient thoughts and questions stemmed from my Sunday school and nursing school students which ultimately led me to conduct research. While teaching, my philosophy (adopted from my husband) is to *teach and you too shall learn.*

Listening and respecting all is a must. Several times while feeling disgruntled and perplexed, God sent a Word through child to uplift me. No matter where one may be God can and will use anyone, anywhere, and anytime, to inspire you for He is Omnipresence (His ability to be everywhere at all times) which is the unlimited nature of God (Ps 139:7-12). While attending my residencies in two different states, God was with me (Thank you Lord) and humbled me while employing the fruit of the spirit. The fruit of the spirit: love, joy, peace, gentleness, goodness, and faith was learned from youth to present and *by the grace and mercy of God* increases daily in my life through continuous prayer. Thank you God for enhancing the fruit of the spirit in my life while on this tedious journey.

Each fruit of the Spirit was significantly employed while completing the *21 pre-requisite courses* (approximately three years) of the doctoral program; for the challenges were immense in dealing with individuals during group assignments. Challenges were even greater throughout the completion of the dissertation. One course in particular (statistics) really challenged my intellect. Because this course was astounding, my niece (Dawnita) was contacted regarding assistance needed (thank you so very much, dear niece). Working together, while challenging various statistical problems resulted in positive retention of the some statistical measures. Moreover since my niece had a very demanding schedule (also enrolled in a doctoral program) my brother Demetrius was consulted for further assistance with statistics.

Thank God for my brother (Pastor Dr. Demetrius Ford) for taking time out of his busy schedule to assist me. Wow, my brother was very good with statistics; but apparently he was extremely thirsty, or just simply loved my Kool-aide. My dear brother drank about five tall glasses of Kool-aide without missing a beat while disseminating the statistical procedures and rationales. While my legs weaken from running back and forth to the kitchen to refill his glass much knowledge was gained. The tutoring from both my niece and brother significantly assisted in pulling me through my statistics class (thank you Lord). Now finished with the pre-requisites and a mentor/committee team all lined-up, preparation was made to complete my *proposal* (first three chapters of my dissertation) in pursuit of approval from the Academic Review Board (ARB) and Internal Review Board (IRB) which would grant me the authority to conduct my research.

CHAPTER 6
EXPECT THE UNEXPECTED

    Beyond belief, is an understatement in regards to this tedious task of pursuing my doctoral degree. Before receiving approval from ARB numerous unexpected things happened. First was the loss of a mentor which took a great period of time seeking and gaining a new one, and the loss of two committee members causing even more lapse in time which resulted in a longer completion date. In addition, countless trips to physicians' offices and emergency rooms (non-compliance with follow-ups) occurred because of my disbelief in the repetitive diagnosis of stress from my primary care physician.

    Of course the diagnosis of severe stress was disingenuous (my perception) and was soon written off. According to my primary care physician my diagnosis deemed me as a candidate for a nervous break-down or stroke; but this would never be voiced on my part. For the most part, multitasking was part of my genetic make-up. Yet, physical and emotional stress was eminent and reflected internal as well as external. One prominent stressor was my glory (hair) falling out in full forces. Help *me Lord (*crying like a baby), *Lord, please, not my hair.* Even a wide-tooth comb was enemy to my hair; for upon combing wads of hair falling out would follow. Subsequently, inferiority was felt because of this major reduction in my covering.

Now what was one to do? Incidentally, my glory was loved for it was non-problematic until now. 1st Corinthians 11:15 reminds one concerning the value of a woman' hair, "But if a woman have long hair, it is a glory to her: for her hair is given her for a covering." Reflecting back, the voice of my father was heard concerning women' glory while in the pulpit (he often used humor before his sermon) saying, *man is God's glory, a woman is man's glory, and a woman's hair is her glory (*1st Corinthians 11:7)*, and if she does not have any hair she will show go out and buy some.* Well, this sound feasible to me, so expediently a trip was made to the beauty supply store to purchase me some glory. While not feeling mentally content with purchasing a full head of hair, my outward appearance was sufficient.

Another external aftermath of my stressors was facial acne accompanied by disfiguration. For acne was never an issue until now, and being so distinct one could argue my face resembled a massive face-lift gone dire. The intensity of the acne and the disfiguring of my face caused another wasted visit to the emergency room, for the physicians' findings was inconclusive (claimed they had never seen anything like this). In fact, the physician added fuel to the fire (increasing my stressors) by returning with several residents to assess my face (now feeling like a freak show character).

What a wasted trip, since no remediation was given and the prescription given did not improve my condition. Now, forthcoming was prayer in asking God to help me and my disfigured face, for being seen in public with a disfigured face was embarrassing to say the least. Howbeit, this incident resulted in missing the upcoming Sunday church services and work. Determined not to miss another church service or work days my remedy was simply going back to the basics (employing plain petroleum) while vowing not to worry about nay sayers questioning what happen to my face. Although years passed, my face was still unhealed yet endeavors' continued.

Moving Forward

Continuing to feel extremely fatigue, thoughts pondered mentally on wishing the doctoral program was never started. Failure deliberated in my weary mind so strongly the thought of departing and moving to another State (remaining unknown and waddling in self-pity and defeat) sound like the perfect remedy. However, my inner spirit would again pose questions and answers such as; you have never let anything defeat you before, are you doubting God? God did not bring you this far to leave you, this task is nothing in the eyesight of God in allowing you to complete. Then of course the ultimate response summoned me; you have invested too much money and time into this degree to walk away.

    Still ambivalent concerning my inner thoughts, the fact remained; it was time to move forward. Yet, my fatigued body was not ready and now stressors reflected inwardly. While lingering in bed waddling in self-pity the aftermath resulted in a loss of appetite. Seriously, one could contend the emergency room was now my best friend (help me Lord). The diagnosis of this visit was dehydration and electrolyte imbalance. After dropping two dress sizes it was a known fact the doctoral program and the excessive obligations (as requirements) were taking a toil.

    The continuous process of my dissertation going back and forth (from my mentor to my committee members and to me for revisions) was greatly challenging and was now physically and emotionally increasing my stress levels. Frequent typing (never was a typist) worsened my current diagnosis of bilateral carpal tunnel syndrome leading to multiple visits to the orthopedic surgeon for steroid injections just for my hands to remain operational. The after effects of being burned-out caused my overall state of mind to drift. Often while attending various functions people would ask, *Juanita, are you feeling alright?* In denial, my answer was always, *I'm fine thank you, just a little tired,* as procedures continued in relationship to my doctoral project.

    Finally, approval was established by ARB and IRB which granted permission to start my research project (Thank you Lord). One day while assembling my 500 survey packages in preparation of mailing them, my sister (Evangelist Theresa Skinner) arrived to drop off a financial donation (bless you my dear sister) but was almost in tears when she looked at my face and stated, *I think this is too much for you, I love you and I don't want to see you going through this!* Knowing she had my best interest at heart, reassurance was given and she went on her way. My sister did not recognize my unconquerable mode and my position of fighting too hard and coming too far to turn back.

Deep down inside my brain, body muscles, and bones were extremely tried. Nevertheless the battle was not over although; my feelings concerning quitting became more intense; the same holds the thoughts of being a failure. Erratically, a soft voice whispered inwardly stating, *there is no failure in your God whom you confess to believe in and depend on.* Generally, when overwhelming thoughts of quitting and failure clutters my mind, reading Bible scriptures tend to reverse this process. One of my favorite scriptures reads (now in scripted and tapped on my laptop), "I can do all things through Christ which strengtheneth me" (Philippians 4:13).

Repeatedly, this scripture was read for the sole purpose of gaining strength and encouragement. For the most part, reading any Biblical literature lifts my spirits and gradually my strength returns. Yet upon returning to tackle my doctoral project the weakness revisited. Now it was time for self-examination as to what in my code of behavior was wrong? Foolishly thinking, Christians striving in their endeavors while being obedience to God (to their best ability) should not be struggling and feeling discontented.

Although depressed (now acknowledging) yet remaining Biblically astute, there was no doubt in my mind that God could change my situation in a blink of an eye? The question surfaced whether there were beans in my eyes blinding me from some erroneous matter on my part? Re-evaluation took place: attending church and rendering services, caring for my family and friends, obedient to God and those commissioned to have authority over me to the best of my ability. Unquestionable, my tithes (*first fruits: gross pay*) and offerings were paid according to the Bible, "Honour the LORD with thy substance, and with the firstfruits of all thine increase; So shall thy barns be filled with plenty, and thy presses shall burst out with new wine" (Proverbs 3:9-10).

Flabbergasted at this point was an understatement in addition to my body being extremely drained and feeble. After working exceedingly hard on this project my body felt like a Hebrew slave (Exodus 1:8-14) working under Pharaoh. Thoughts of what was hindering me continued to ruminate and my mind was now conditioned to pray for faith, strength, and understanding. In making matters worse, one would question me if, *I had bit off more than I could chew?* While this comment pierced my heart, inadvertently a burst of energy emerged which caused me to work even harder. In addition to working harder more time was spent reading my Bible and while reading my Bible God led me to several noteworthy powerful passages of scriptures that would change my life.

The first passage was, "God is our refuge and strength, a very present help in trouble. Therefore we will not fear, Even though the earth be removed, and though the mountains be carried into the midst of the sea; Though its waters roar and be troubled, though the mountains shake with its swelling. Selah" (Psalm 46:1-3). The second passages of scriptures were "Casting all your care upon him; for he careth for you" (1st Peter 5:7), and the third scripture was, ". . . Thus saith the LORD unto you, Be not afraid nor dismayed by reason of this great multitude; for the battle is not yours, but God's" (2nd Chronicles 20:15). Fervently praying my plea was for God to assist me in knowing His voice and to give me understanding of his word, and He did. Not surprising, the concept of what God was trying to envision in me was now comprehended (*Thank you Jesus*).

God in turn revealed to me what was wrong; although putting my best foot forward, working hard, and being obedient, my faith wavered and there was no total submission of my doctoral project to him. The nerve of thinking this task could be accomplished on my own and in my own time span was fallible. While demonstrating humbleness to my committee members a rush was commissioned to God because of extreme fatigue. Now fully surrendering my dissertation project over to God, prayers of gratefulness, forgiveness, and the need for *grace, mercy*, and favor commenced.

While instigating my prayer (tears flooded my eyes and saturated my upper clothing) and God was summoned like never before. Pouring out my heart, pleading began with forgiveness for being impatience, selfish, and for not fully trusting him. Reverence was given in recognition of my God's powerfulness (*Omnipotence*) and acknowledgement in knowing how things could turn around in my favored whenever He desired. My heavenly Father was petitioned regarding my weariness and how the doctoral project was weighing heavy on my heart. An appeal was made to my Father on how my doctoral project was now surrendered over to Him. My prayer to my Savior was, if this project was going to change me from being humble and cause my eyes to turn from Him to take it away. In closing, my prayer reverenced my Father for knowing my heart and my desires (*Omniscient*), and my prayer ended with a salutation, if this project completion is *not* your will then let your will be done. My doxology to God was that the worrying was no longer mine because my trust and belief is in you Father, for you know my desires, what's best for me, and wherever this road leads me (*Omnipresent*) you know my destiny.

Surprising, were the thoughts that expediently accumulated in my mind while praying; for thoughts had never swiftly surfaced before while praying to God. My conclusion was that the Holy Spirit (Jesus) had made intercessory prayers on my behalf. Romans 8: 26-27 confirmed my thought by stating, "Likewise the Spirit also helpeth our infirmities: for we know not what we should pray for as we ought: but the Spirit itself maketh intercession for us with groanings which cannot be uttered; And he that searcheth the hearts knoweth what is the mind of the Spirit, because he maketh intercession for the saints according to the will of God."

After praying my spirit was that of a new person. My new vows were to get out more often and spend more time with my family while continuing to work on my doctoral project. Soon respondents' completed surveys returned, data was interpreted/analyzed, and completion of the last two chapters (now called the Dissertation; total five chapters) was now on the way. This process involved the hiring of editors and statisticians (costly), but God provided the means. Finally my dissertation was completed and was submitted to the Institutional Review Board (IRB) for approval. After several revisions and completion of this long and tedious process my approval came which granted permission for my oral defense to take place (Praise God, thank you Father).

The *Oral Defense* called for a verbal dissemination and defense of my dissertation to my committee members which included a synopsis concerning: the dissertation, statistical procedures/results, and the research significance to the body of nursing and other organizations in approximately 30-45 minutes. Upon completion of my defense the committee members posed questions concerning various aspects of my dissertation (their area of choice). Although extremely anxious and uneasy, God carried me through (praise *the Lord)* and results of my oral defense were the approved status.

Bless God's Holy Name, another milestone completed, but the process was not over. Now final editing of the dissertation took place before submission to the Dean of the University. Disappointing, was the return (Not Approved) this project would take another year before completion. The proverbial phrase *patience is a virtue* has now become one of my desired qualities (*Lord help me to hold out while persevering*).

Again the process of strict editing and revising (particularly statistics) took place. The concept of nurse burnout was an understatement often triggering me to feel victimized as voiced by some relatives and friends. Again my spirit was low and my thoughts of fighting a losing battle challenged me. Yes, negative connotations were assigned by some. One must remember not all who say they love you are truly for you or hold your best interest at heart. All the same, my spiritual nature knew who to turn this battle over too. For comforting my sole could only be provided by my heavenly Father and only He could keep me with a sound mind while remaining focused on completing this task. Isaiah 66:13 reminded me, "As one whom his mother comforteth, so will I comfort you. . .", and God did according to His Word.

Experiencing the Grace and Mercy of God

Now steadfast and focused, revisions of my dissertation continued and God supplied all the assistance needed. While feeling more positive, another stagnated problem derived with my statistics. However, before the panic mode surfaced God already had the master plan waiting to be employed on my behalf. If one ever dealt with statisticians then one knows how costly and busy statisticians can be. At this time of need my past two statisticians were too busy to assist me. Staying focused, for some reason there were no concerns regarding the cost of the needed statistician, on the contrary my focus was on finding another good statistician and gaining more work hours to offset the cost. Miraculously, by *the Grace and Mercy of God* one of my committee members referred me to an excellent statistician. In fact, my committee member was so adamant concerning this statistician working with me his exact words were; you *tell him I referred you* (Praise God).

After receiving the statistician's name, my eyes denoted his initials being the same as mine, and my Lord and Savior (J.C.) prompting me to feel even more positive concerning his expertise as a statistician. After thanking and praising God for sending this statistician in my path a called was placed to speak with him. The statistician was kind, humble, and treated me with respect. Humbly, my thoughts were this man was another angel sent by God to assist me throughout the approval process. His steadfast and robust persona was very welcoming, it was as if he felt my frustrations and knew of my weakness (physically and emotionally). Once again, my dissertation was in a state of major revisions (mainly the statistical analysis section). As the year progressed all revisions were completed and my third submission to the Dean of the University was on the way.

Praise God Almighty; finally a break from writing the dissertation while waiting to hear feedback from the Dean. In an effort of deterring my mind of the anxiety imbedded inside while waiting on the Dean's results, other affairs were attended too. Daily tasks at home, working two part-time jobs, spending more quality time with family members, and the excitement of planning to attend my two older daughters' (Kimberly Rebecca Campbell and Franita Kenyatta Gathings) graduation from their Master's Programs (Thank you Lord). Indeed it is a blessing as well as a privilege to be able to spend quality time with one's biological and spiritual families.

Several months passed and while grocery shopping with my sister (Wanda) a strange call was received from my Academic Counselor from the University addressing me as Dr. *Crawford*. How strange this call was, nonetheless, the caller was corrected by me informing him of being premature with the title since my results from the Dean had not been received. The caller was apologetic and stated he would call at a later date. Still feeling astonished regarding the call my sister was informed. Her reply was *what? Nevertheless,* we proceeded to finish shopping.

Still puzzled concerning the call from my Academic Counselor, a voice spoke to me and said; *check your email upon returning home*. Although anxious, my mind was made up *not* to become upset no matter what. My thoughts were to return home, put up the groceries, and rush to check my emails. Well, there were no emails from my Mentor or committee members, but wait (have mercy Lord); there was one email from the Dean of the University. After panicking and feeling uneasy, God was petitioned in prayer to just hold me and let me be content with whatever the Deans' remarks and recommendations were.

Subsequent to taking a deep breath, the email was opened and to my amazement *it was finished*. God was petitioned in prayers of thanksgivings, falling on my knees with a joyful cry praises begin in thanking God and my Lord and Savior as to what was just read! The email stated, *Congratulations Dr. Juanita Crawford (EDD), your dissertation has been approved*, and that was enough for me. Incidentally, the EDD stands for *Educational Doctorate Degree* or simply *Doctor of Education;* not to be mistaken for Medical Doctor (MD). Now stunned, ecstatic, and in disbelief (knowing this task was finally over), my mind was anesthetized to the point of not knowing what to do. Praises continued to God and my Lord and Savior. Meditation took place on all the assistance (mentor, committee members, statisticians, editors, family, and friends) my heavenly Father sent on my behalf. A moment of deliberation took place regarding my stressors and aftermath of the stress.

A special prayer was petitioned for all who encouraged and assisted (financially, emotionally, and prayerfully) me in completion of this task. My very last reflection was again on my heavenly Father whom was thanked and praised over and over. After clearing my now puffed-up watery eyes and choked-up throat my husband was informed who became even more ecstatic (*bless him*). In fact, before getting a chance to call and inform my family members, my husband proceeded to call first. Truly, this verdict was a blessing to me and all others praying and rooting on my behalf throughout this *six year tedious journey* (Thank you all).

Noticeably, my body, mind, soul, and spirit felt relieved. Praise God, *Jehovah Nissi* (The Lord is my Banner; Exodus 17: 15-16), which means *marked victory*. Because of the exhaustion from the program my thoughts were not to attend the graduation ceremony, but this would not stand in regards to my husband who appealed to me to attend on his behalf. His request was honored on the grounds he purchase my Doctoral Regalia. Surely he accepted the grounds but may have wanted to retract this decision upon learning the Doctoral Regalia was well over $700 (h*elp us Jesus*). Not in a lifetime would he retract on this decision; after all he tells me this was his degree as well. This gift from my husband was very appreciative, for the robe is beautiful (resembling a Bishop's Robe).

Surprisingly, while in attendance at the graduation the doctoral candidates were treated in high regards from all (including other graduates candidates). While remaining humble and feeling privileged, my prayers continued in thanking God for His blessings and strengthening me in the area of patience. For out of well over *1000* graduates (seven doctorates) *yours truly* was the last one to be called and hooded on stage. My thoughts of this scenario led me to the morals of Matthew 20:16 in which Jesus is speaking on laborers in the vineyard, "So the last shall be first, and the first last. . .", which in my humble opinion denotes, by *Grace (not merit)*, regardless of how much time is served by Christians, we all will receive our rewards according to God's will. In heaven, no one can assert (regardless of your status on earth) a special honor, for all are equally special to God. Praise God for allowing me be His servant as a parishioner and thank you Father, in the Name of Our Lord and Savior Jesus Christ for your *Grace and Mercy*.

CHAPTER 7
RENDERING SERVICES

Graduation Day was wonderful and is now over, the final chapter of my dissertation is completed and this research book is closed. Intermittently In 2011, God graciously blessed my youngest daughter Ronda Latricia Suthers (AKA: Precious) to graduate with here Associate Degree in Science (Praise God). Again the question arises, as stated in Psalm 116:12, "What shall I render unto the Lord for all of His benefits towards me?" Howbeit God does not need anyone or anything; in fact, everything belongs to and was made by God! As stated in Psalms 50: 10-12 concerning God's Majesty, "For every beast of the forest is mine, and the cattle upon a thousand hills. I know all the fowls of the mountains: and the wild beasts of the field are mine. If I were hungry, I would not tell thee: for the world is mine, and the fullness thereof." Consequently, the answer to this question (What shall I render unto the Lord for all of His benefits towards me) is simple, no one can reimburse the Lord.

On a personal note, my Supreme God in waking me up this morning, supplying food to offset my hunger, allowing me to breath His air , permitting my taste buds to remain active, letting my limbs move effectively (often taken for granted), and watching over me and my family in a world of turmoil can never be repaid. No, my Heavenly Father can never be reimbursed for guiding and protecting me and my family as we travel back and forth to our destinations without incidents, clothing me in my desired fashion (yes, I love to dress), and consenting my body as healthy (even after inputting toxins) when the doctors voiced the contrary.

It is impossible to repay God for: blessing me with multiple gifts, placing individuals in my paths to assist in my endeavors, inspiring me to write this personal book, and imbedding me with a heart to love and the desire to help anyone in need. My biggest desire is to help and encourage others to come to Christ for a better life and to live eternality. God is good, God is gracious, God is merciful, and worthy to be praised, yet no one can repay him.

Looking back over my life God has been truly good to me and while many voiced that my struggle down this path would not triumph, God spoke it into existence. For it was God who carried me through this terminal degree tedious journey, and placed the necessary individuals in my path. Through it all God saw fit for a little old servant like me to make it through. Often while opting to fail or bail out God lifted me up. For "When I said, my foot slippeth; thy mercy, O Lord, held me up. In the multitude of my thoughts within me thy comforts delight my soul (Psalms 94:18-19). Unquestionably, my praise to God will be to no end and services will be rendered unto Him in all aspects of my life ". . . for unto whomsoever much is given, of him shall be much required . . ." (Luke 12:48). Yes, my soul loves the Lord, He heard my cry and came to my rescue and for this my praises and thanks to Him will forever continue, bless His Holy name. My prayer is assist others in coming to know and honor my Father and my Lord and Savior Jesus Christ for a greater future.

The Appeal
All can honor God by accepting His son Jesus Christ as your personal Savior, be baptized, remain obedient to his word, keep the faith, and continue to glorify him. Yet, one must remember that in being a Christian by no means are we perfect or immune from challenges, trials or tribulations ; for God rains on the just as well as the unjust (Matthew 5:45) and as parents love and chasten their children when they falter so will God chasten. Revelations 3:19 states, "As many as I love, I rebuke and chasten: be zealous therefore, and repent." Neither, are Christians exempted from being provoked to anger or feeling weak at times, yet Apostle Paul states, his . . . "grace is sufficient for thee: for my strength is made perfect in weakness . . ." (2nd Corinthians 12:9). Still, without a doubt one is better off being a Christian verses *being of this world* for God will never fail you as individuals but this world will. The

truth of the matter is, "if God be for us, who can be against us?" (Romans 8:31).

While this earthly travel can be very daunting and challenging, there is a Savior by the name of Jesus Christ who can make your road brighter and your load lighter. He is standing at your door knocking waiting to be let in. Jesus is the only one, who can give you contentment when the bills are due and the finances are low; when the refrigerator is empty and the children are hungry, and when you are surrounded by trouble and there's nowhere to run; he will take care of you. My appeal to all is that God is the *Only* pre-eminent (supreme, best, absolute; Revelation 17:14) God, and Jesus Christ (His son) is Lord of Lords and the King of Kings, and if one freely come unto him, bow down in prayer and repent, he will lift them up (Psalms 145:14). Jesus Christ is a comforter; after losing my father, mother, sister, and brother, my testimony is that Jesus is the only one who can effectively comfort you in your time of sorrow (Psalms 34:18). He will be a father to the fatherless (Psalms 68:5). Jesus will always be with you and will continue to strengthen you when all others have departed.

One must learn to lean and depend on God as your everlasting Father (thank you Lord). "Hast thou not known? Hast thou not heard that the everlasting God, the LORD, the Creator of the ends of the earth, fainteth not, neither is weary? There is no searching of his understanding. He giveth power to the faint; and to them that have no might he increaseth strength. Even the youths shall faint and be weary, and the young men shall utterly fall: But they that wait upon the LORD shall renew their strength; they shall mount up with wings as eagles; they shall run, and not be weary; and they shall walk, and not faint" (Isaiah 40:28-31).

God is my all-in-all; this statement is a true indication because throughout my life and endeavors the mighty hand of God watched over and protected me. My endorsement is that God will make a way out of a way (yes, God always have a way). Therefore, my petition is to continue rendering my heart and soul unto the Lord. As stated in Psalm 138:1-3, "I will praise thee with my whole heart . . . In the day when I cried thou answeredst me, and strengthenedst me with strength in my soul."

Conclusions

God want each and every one of us to have a benevolent heart and to be submissive to His will. Upon conviction of our sins and the acceptance of Jesus Christ as our Lord and Savior, we must be obedient in an effort to please him. Our Father in heaven gave his only begotten son Jesus Christ who shed His Blood as atonement for our sins because he loves us. For, it was not the nails that held Jesus to the cross, it was love. Jesus stated in Matthew 10:11, "I am the good shepherd: the good shepherd giveth his life for the sheep." Need we be reminded; Jesus did not have to give up his life for us, he could have fought and won his captive. Jesus stated in Matthew 26: 53, "Thinkest thou that I cannot now pray to my Father, and he shall presently give me more than twelve legions of angels?"

Jesus goes on to say, "No man taketh it from me, but I lay it down of myself. I have power to lay it down, and I have power to take it again. This commandment have I received of my Father" (John 10:18).

All God wants of His children in return is our hearts, minds, and commitment to serve him eternally. God is the only one who can meet all of our needs, if we only trust Him. My appeal is to all who have not given their lives over to Jesus Christ, to make a change today. In being a living witness my acknowledgment is that God can and will change anyone who desire to change (upon submission to Him). Yes, God is longsuffering, but invite him now while the blood is running warm in your veins and the opportunity to choose righteousness is still accessible; for God in his own time will release them that remain disobedient. Romans 27:28 states, "And even as they did not like to retain God in their knowledge, God gave them over to a reprobate mind . . ."

My appeal is for the unsaved to repent, be baptized, magnify the lord (2nd Peter 3:9) and continue your faith in God. Never turn from your First Love (God) to consign to a job, school, family, friends, a business, etc., making these your ultimate gods. God is a jealous God as stated in Deuteronomy 6:14-16, "Ye shall not go after other gods, of the gods of the people which are round about you; For the LORD thy God is a jealous God among you lest the anger of the LORD thy God be kindled against thee, and destroy thee from off the face of the earth." One must remember that God is our maker and allows us to partake in all of our endeavors and in a twinkling of an eye (1st Corinthians 15:52) God can change things. When you are faced with calamities, the prudent man runs to the church and not from the church.

Be not afraid to stand up for God and do not fret when one challenge or threaten you. God will take care of you, for when one door closes God is already in the plan opening others. Stay close to positive individuals who inspire and encourage you. Always give honor unto whom honor is due (Romans 13:7). Wake up each morning with gladness, giving thanks, and praises unto our Lord and Savior for allowing you to see another day. Take off the woe- it's- me or self-pity mentality, stop blaming others for your failure or mistakes; for there is no failure in God but in man. God knows everyone that has mistreated you, for he knows the number of hairs on your head (Luke 12:7) and he will take what one employed for your destruction and employ it for your good (Genesis 50:20).

Take the step of faith leaving the past behind while focusing on God's blessing ahead. Stay steadfast in the Lord and he will give you the desires of your heart. John 15:7 states, "If ye abide in me, and my words abide in you, ye shall ask what ye will, and it shall be done unto you. When striving to accomplish any endeavor remember this scripture, "I can do all things through Christ which strengtheneth me" (Philippians 4:13). The spirit of God dwelleth in you (Romans 8:11), keep the Faith and God will empower you. My intent is to petition all concerning the love of God and to let all know that God considers all of His children precious and there is deliverance through His son, our Lord and Savior Jesus Christ. My evidence is that Jesus delivered an old wrench like me regardless of my faults and imperfections, so why not you? This is my confession regardless to how others perceive me, for James 5:16 posits, "Confess your faults one to another, and pray one for another, that ye may be healed ..." For it's not important what people think of you, but what God thinks of you.

My appeal is to all because God has worked many miracles throughout my life and it is my *solemn duty* to inform, encourage, and empower all to find relief and strength in Jesus Christ. Jesus after casting out demons in a man (Legion) whom dwelled in the tombs instructed him to " . . . Go home to thy friends, and tell them how great things the Lord hath done for thee, and hath had compassion on thee. And he departed, and began to publish in Decap'olis how great things Jesus had done for him: and all *men* did marvel" (Mark 5:19-20). One must remember after becoming a born again Christian God changes you from the old person to a new one; do not entertain when one is quick to bring up your past. "Therefore if any man be in Christ, he is a new creature: old things are passed away; behold all things are become new. And all things are of God" (2nd Corinthians 5:17). You are who God says you are; never depend on what you know but who you know (Jesus).

God takes pride in prospering his children and made us heirs. Romans 8:16-18 reads, "The Spirit itself beareth witness with our spirit, that we are the children of God: And if children, then heirs; heirs of God, and joint-heirs with Christ; if so be that we suffer with him, that we may be also glorified together. For I reckon that the sufferings of this present time are not worthy to be compared with the glory which shall be revealed in us." In all endeavors, never lose hope, "For we are saved by hope: but hope that is seen is not hope: for what a man seeth, why doth he yet hope for? But if we hope for that we see not, then do we with patience wait for it" (Romans 8:24-25).

A Hymn writer by the name of Rev. Edward Mote (Baptist Pastor, born in 1797) was the initial author of the hymn *My Hope is Built: The Solid Rock*. Mote wrote this song in 1834 and the song was first printed in a Spiritual Magazine in 1837. The writer wrote this hymn as a reflection of 'Gracious experiences of a Christian.' Rev. Mote was asked by a friend to visit his gravely-ill wife. Prior to praying for his friends' wife this hymn was sung and because she enjoyed it, he decided to publish it.

Two of my favorite verses of this hymn are:

> ♪ *"My hope is built on nothing less Than Jesus' blood and righteousness. I dare not trust the sweetest frame, but wholly trust in Jesus' Name.*
>
> ♪ *When He shall come with trumpet sound, oh may I then in Him be found.*

Dressed in His righteousness alone, faultless to stand before the throne!"

(Net Hymnal (2011)

    Many churches nationwide sing this hymn and I concur with the lyrics. Romans 15, 1:4 confirms the importance of remaining hopeful, "For whatsoever things were written aforetime were written for our learning, that we through patience and comfort of the scriptures might have hope."

    Yes one must remain hopeful, for God wants his children to excel in all endeavors and we must learn to trust that God has our best interest at heart. We may not know what the future holds for us, but we know who holds our future. Jeremiah 29:11 states, "For I know the plans I have for you," declares the LORD, "plans to prosper you and not to harm you, plans to give you hope and a future" (New International Version). To all individuals reading this book my prayer is that through God's *Grace and Mercy* you will gain insight, hindsight, and foresight of what God's miraculous Agape love can and will do for you, if you let Him lead you. "Now unto him that is able to do exceeding abundantly above all that we ask or think, according to the power that worketh in us. Unto him be glory in the church by Christ Jesus throughout all ages, world without end. Amen." (Ephesians 3:20-21).

Agape, Dr. Juanita Crawford, Ed.D., MSN, RN

REFERENCES

Bauman, K.J., & Graf, N. F. (August, 2003). *U.S. Department of Commerce: Economics and Statistics Administration: U.S. CENSUS BUREAU*. Retrieved January 14, 2013 from http://www.census.gov/prod/2003pubs/c2kbr-24.pdf

Net Hymnal. (2011). My hope is built: The solid rock. *Cyberhymnal*. Retreived April 28, 2013 from http://cyberhymnal.org/htm/m/y/myhopeis.htm

The Blue Book. (n.d.). Have thine own way. *Free online library*. Retrieved May 3, 2013 from http://library.timelesstruths.org/music/Have_Thine_Own_Way_Lord/

The Holy Bible. (2011). New International Version. *Biblica, Inc*. Retrieved April 12, 2013, from http://www.biblegateway.com/passage/?search=Matthew%2020:4&version=NIV

The Holy Bible. (1998). *King James Version. Large print compact edition*. Holman Bible Publishers: Korea.

Wikipedia. (2012, October). *Have thine own way, Lord*. Wikipedia: The free encyclopedia. Retrieved May 3, 2013 from http://en.wikipedia.org/wiki/Have_Thine_Own_Way,_Lord

About The Author

Dr. Juanita Crawford was deferred for her Doctor of Education Degree on June 23, 2010 and is an Adjunct Nursing Professor. Hobbies include singing, reading, and spending quality with her family.

www.ingramcontent.com/pod-product-compliance
Lightning Source LLC
Chambersburg PA
CBHW070653050426
42451CB00008B/334